SUI
CIDE

Suicide

By

Machelle S. Jemison

First edition

Advisor: Lorieen Henry

Beloved,

It is much easier to love what is yours thank to long after what use to be. It was in my greatest moments of darkness and transparency; I came face to face with what will forever be my greatest betrayal. This betrayal is not

because you betrayed me, but because I betrayed myself in returning to the "love" you displayed was toxic to me. You didn't fail me. I failed me when I believed you were more than what you had shown yourself to be. I dedicate this book to me because I forgive me.

Table Of Contents

Preface

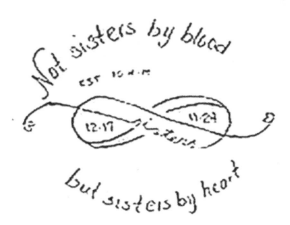

Not sisters by blood
csr 10.4.11
12.17   11.21
but sisters by heart

Beloved,

I dedicate this book to you as an offer of love; an official apology, and a release of forgiveness to you. I also offer forgiveness to myself for not responding to the clarion call of God when HE made a way of escape for me. However, our love is forever. Always has been. Always will be. The integrity of my love is rooted in the love of GOD.

Even my own close friend in whom I trusted, who ate my bread, has lifted up his heel against me [in betrayal]. But You, O Lord, be gracious to me and restore me [to health], so that I may repay them. By this, I know that you favor and delight in me, because my enemy does not shout in triumph over me. As for me, you uphold me in my integrity, and you set me in your presence forever. Blessed be the Lord, the God of Israel, From everlasting to everlasting [from this age to the next, and forever]. Amen and Amen (so be it).

Psalms 41:9-13 AMP

If it were not for you and this brokenness experienced, I don't know that I could have ever reached this place of wisdom, knowledge, understanding, compassion, empathy, and best of all self-love. I have said this before, and I will say it now for all to see – you taught me to love. Before you, I was hurt before, but I have never been willing to put my all into another person, because I never trusted anyone to do anything more than hurt me.

You, however, were different. We bonded in brokenness and let our guards down together, and because I let my guard down in a way like never before, you were able to hurt me to a depth I never knew existed. You told me I was the first to ever love you the way you want to be loved and I told you I don't want to love, but for you I was willing to try. I tried it. I loved it. Moreover, I am forever grateful for who you are and I pray that God reigns manna from heaven on you that your storeroom is filled and you never find that place of emptiness again. Forever will I love you.

May God's peace that surpasses all understanding be with you.

Seleda

Acknowledgements

What is understood never requires an explanation.

Sinamen Nixon

Lorieen Henry

Ned Watson

Thank you, Dr. Florencia Sellers

Your decades of hard work and dedication to prayer, fasting, encouraging, and all of the many things that you have taught me about endurance have not gone unnoticed. I believe that Jesus was strategic in His choosing of the disciples – Colossians 4.14 our dear friend Luke, the doctor, and Demas send greetings. I am glad that Jesus has also given me – a beloved physician – in this journey of life.

Offended

I f you would, for just a moment's time, allow me to share my heart with you. Let me paint this picture for you – I am in this confessional as I seek godly counsel that I might heal. In the Psalms of David, he tells us, Oh, the joys of those who do not follow the advice of the wicked, or stand around with sinners, or join in with mockers. Though my mind desired to plot revenge, my heart sought godly counsel that I may return to the purposeful plan for my life. We all make mistakes and I had gone wayward and entered a life of sin that would be a change in me forever.

Father, God, in the name of Jesus, we come before you as humble as we know how, thanking you for your Grace and MERCY towards all mankind. Father, we repent of any sins committed against you, knowingly and unknowingly, let the words out of our mouths be acceptable in your sight. Father, we thank you for being the Abba of our lives, showing us your ways and making our lives line up with your word. Father, thank you for your love that we have freely been able to give; and thank you for the heart of man.

We ask you to protect, restore, revive and mold us to reflect your perfect will while giving us clarity on what is required from us without compromising you. God, we love and thank you for the Holy Spirit. Allow your presence to captivate our minds, bodies and soul. Show us what is needed and allow love to flow. Allow the elevation in this place to shift the atmosphere over the enemy. We bind up any demonic force that is not of you; Lord I ask that your consuming fire burn off all purities and allow the blood of the Lamb to cover your children, and that no weapon formed against us will prosper, not even the biggest fears we have within ourselves! We thank you for a cleansed mind and refreshed anointing that will love despite rejection or abandonment.

Despite the fear of being gay, for our hearts and minds rest in you that you may fill every void with your perfect purpose, mold us, oh God, and continue to shower our kids with discipline, love compassion, wisdom, knowledge, understanding and a discerning spirit to only follow Christ in the mist of the unknown. Show your face God and instruct us on how to love and be loved without compromising or inserting ourselves in anything outside of your will. Use us today to shower light into darkness and welcome many souls to you - that you get all the glory. Protect us as we travel and protect us as we chase after you. For you are Alpha and Omega, this work you started in us you will be the one to finish, and I ask for strength, endurance, perseverance, wisdom, and a discerning spirit to know and trust you outside of what I can see or feel. We love you and thank you! Hallelujah, Hallelujah Hallelujah, Amen.

ALJ

She preys.

Prayer was one of the ways that I found were key to my heart until I realized that this was an easy way to get me off my guard. It was the endless prayer and what seemed to be loyalty that slowly, but surely, caused me to relax. It's never a good idea to start in the middle of a story, but this is my story and we will travel from the middle to the end and somehow reach the beginning from there. She prays for me, or did she prey on me? Only she and God knows the intent of all that she went through to break barriers to get me to trust her and lead me to this place of abandonment that was common ground for us both.

I completely understand when the songwriter said I kissed a girl and I liked it. I mean, this girl was me with a different edge to her. She was edgy, strong, kind of witty, but she had this ghetto bougie thing going that made her most interesting to me. It was something that I loved, but I knew I could never take home to my folks. I mean, hell, I didn't even want to take her home to my folks. She wasn't my little secret, but she wasn't my girlfriend either.

This situation was complex because there is something in me that, at times, craves a sense of excitement. She excited the shit out of me. She spoke to the parts of me that I was afraid to let others see. People have gotten so accustomed to me being strong that at any sign of weakness, they are praying for my healing. I had been a single parent at our meeting for 14 years and my son didn't even know what it looked like for me to have a moment of weakness. My mental breakdowns, tears cried, thoughts of suicide, and my being overwhelmed all happened in my closet in the middle of the night and I could never allow it to carry over into the morning. People, for some strange reason, are unreceptive of me hurting, being weak, or even having emotion. This chick was the exact opposite. She always reminded me that she needed to see the real me - the behind closed doors me.

If I'm honest with myself, it was so easy to be in love with her despite not wanting a relationship because of its conflict of interest with my religious belief and practices. I mean, I told you before - she prays for me. I can't say beyond doubt that she kept my secrets because I don't know for sure. What I will say is that the things that I was willing to share, I haven't seen them on Facebook yet. Lol.

Bear with me as I laugh and cry through this series of events. In my Will Smith voice - this is the story all about how my life got flipped, turned upside down. This is the ride of a lifetime and with my hands lifted and heart filled with praise, I am blessed by each crazy moment.

Imagine reading this in a text thread.

You: My greatest fear is being the gay they called me for years. So, I don't want to love since we are praying about it.

Her: I understand I can love you. Despite your fears, God's got us!!! Healing means you have to know mother love, sister love, and family love, before you get to that place or any other place where Gay is concerned. If gay is LOVE, THEN WE ALL ARE AMEN.

You: Don't forget to hit me when you get home. Thank you, I needed that.

Her: I won't and thank you, I needed it as well. For me, my biggest fear is more so rejection because of abandonment.

You: I know. I just needed you to say it. No more solo missions, remember?

Her: Realizing I wasn't good enough for my mom and letting someone come in to use that against me. Looking at family like they are not due to the lies that was told to protect me but end causing me unspeakable pain.

The worst connection that you can ever make with someone is one that is founded on past pains. Though you bond and become strong together, one of you will eventually self-sabotage due to the fear of past hurt arising in the new bond being established. I guess I was a little stronger than I thought because her fears caused her to cave and do all the things to me that she was afraid of. That rejection and abandonment that she was so afraid of feeling, she had no problem at all leaving me at the alter to marry that past pain.

The crazy thing is I wasn't feeling too well on a Thursday night, and on this particular night, I don't know if I will ever forget. Before her, I was never much of a cuddler, but with her, it was one of my greatest attributes. I had some really bad stomach pains. She kept trying to get me to go to the emergency room but based on the prayers from my secret place, I knew that pain was for the purpose of getting my attention. We had admitted to falling in love with one another, but I didn't want to be in love with a woman because I am a Christian. I guess it's a little too late with the Christian card because I surely didn't play it before she gave me the best head of my life underwater, and she didn't use hers before we broke that bed competing to be one another's best sex ever. The only person I had told that I had been praying for a move of God was my mentor and she was praying with me because she understood the conflict I was experiencing.

I was hurting in pain, and this was the calm before the storm. She held me, fussed at me about not wanting to go to the doctor, gave me the sweetest kisses, and then took a few phone calls in the closet - in secret, and that changed the dynamics of all that was going on. I was thinking she wasn't just taking private calls in the closet, but she was really a little at a time putting all her belongings in garbage bags. She thought she had secretly moved her kids out days before, but attention to detail is everything. We noticed she was moving and didn't care. Movers came later that morning so all that 'let's go to the hospital,' 'I love you,' 'I'm concerned about you,' was as fake as designer bags from the trunk of the car. She was moving out and lacked the maturity to come to me woman to woman, to tell me she had a problem with me or whatever I had done to make her abruptly move out and create unnecessary drama in doing so. That's for another time though. I guess if you fear rejection enough you become the rejecter; and if there is enough fear of being abandoned then you do just that. Abandon those that are genuinely in your corner. I wasn't even sure if I could tell this story because it's embarrassing. As I've spoken with my mentor for months and months about a variety of things, her best advice was write!

She told me to write; yet I had no words. The condemnation of others was louder in my ear than the encouragement of those who loved me. I have had my fair share of mistakes, none that I am ashamed to admit because they were my choices. Then I made the choice to stay "out of the way" because, while I am not my mistakes, I just lie in silence in the bed of condemnations that others had given me all in the name of Jesus Christ. In my own silence, they told me to write. In my disobedience, I found an excuse that I did not have to deal with the cloud of condemnation that I could not seem to shake. Have you ever been listening to something and it hits you like a ton of bricks? This is what I hear - "The church was not meant for sinners like me; just sinners like you." This spoke volume to me because a pastor was being judged by the board of elders because he had fallen in love with a prostitute that had relapsed with heroin use.

Hosea 3:1-3 MSG

Then God ordered me, "Start all over: Love your wife again, your wife who's in bed with her latest boyfriend, your cheating wife. Love her the way I, God, love the Israelite people, even as they flirt and party with every God that takes their fancy." I did it. I paid good money to get her back. It cost me the price of a slave. Then I told her, "From now on, you're living with me. No more whoring, no more sleeping around. You're living with me and I'm living with you."

This, for me is so amazing because, in Hosea's experience, though this woman "fell" back into her old ways, he pushed through with loving her. Hosea's love mirrored God's love. It goes further to say, "The people of Israel are going to live a long time stripped of security and protection, without religion and comfort, godless and prayerless. But in time they'll come back, these Israelites, come back looking for their God and their King David. They'll come back chastened to reverence before God and his good gifts, ready for the End of the story of his love". Beyond the rape, feeling of abandonment, running from 'the call', married as a sense of protection, divorce, smoking, alcohol, and unfaithfulness to God - He still loved me. So, I went into a place of consecration. I thought to live a clean life, only to fall again. This time was different. I allowed my prayer partner to have sex with me. Can't give away all responsibility, because I made the choice to do it more than once. I spent a lot of time questioning how I ended up with a woman in my bed. Beyond her betrayal, lies, and attempt to slander my name - I still can say I love her. Even better than that, I can still say GOD loves me. Walking away from the Father is the easy road. Staying in sin due to comfort is not unheard of. Returning to the Father is not the easiest thing in the world. Here are my two reasons that returning was difficult:

1. I believe in the word of God; so, I believed that if I confessed my faults, the person I confessed to could pray, and I'd be healed. However, the "this was your fault; you should have known better" mantra made it a little difficult.

2. Though I was not ashamed of my mistakes, knowing that I had confessed to someone that led me to condemnation versus conviction had me questioning years of "prophecy", spiritual gifts, assignments, and worse of all, I questioned if life was worth living.

I knew I messed up. Surely, I didn't need someone else to throw that in my face. The first step to recovery is admitting you have a problem. If I was able to come to you with admission that I have a problem, I have acknowledged I MESSED UP. That wasn't rocket science. When did we get to the place that the church was no longer a place of healing? The four walls of the "church" is where you find that 'saints' create toxic environments, hurt you, manipulate you, make other saints turn against you, preach whole sermons about you to justify how they hurt you, and even embellish the story to make it look worse than it was. I just need to take a minute to thank God that HE got up so that I could get up again. HE just will not allow me to stay in the bed of pity at the hands of others. No matter how much I want to be in hiding, not for shame, but because I don't want to be brutally honest to people, I'm supposed to respect due to their position. I would much rather stay in my own world.

My own world can produce thoughts that are all over the place. One day I'm pondering, how it may be relatable that women return to abusive relationships. I mean, I can never say I don't understand how women keep going back to being abused. Especially not after loving on, being taken advantage of, yet still returning to you. It's been 20 years and we still have this on and off again relationship. Your face changed over the years, yet you remained the same. Who are you? What is your name? We've danced this routine a long time and I still don't know what to call you. For years I called you Dad, then later husband and almost wife. What is it about you that you keep coming back? What is it about me that I don't recognize you when you come? We just pick up where we left off - laughs, cuddles and smiles. It's not common for us to argue but if we do, it's lifechanging. Three huge disagreements. The first two I never saw you again. The last one, you stayed a little longer than before, but things were not the same, so you left anyway. But this last time you left and damaged my soul when you attempted to taint my name and overwhelmed the characteristics, I've attempted to perfect with your lies about who I am. We argued about abortion. You said no one could find out - that our love had to remain a secret because others would be able to comprehend what GOD was allowing us to share. You left and it drove me crazy. I sat on the steps until dark, sometimes awaiting your return. I watched out of the window and listened to see if my phone would ring. We argued about divorce. You told me if I loved you I wouldn't leave you. If I were truly a Christian, I would be accepting and not so judgmental. I remember sitting in that bubble bath, drinking and popping those scripts because the pain was loud and I just needed it to lower its voice. I do love you. I'm not judgmental. I want to be right with GOD and I don't believe in divorce, but I'm not open to receive your love because it's been tainted. You apologized and begged for forgiveness for weeks and at that one moment of weakness, I was ready to forgive while in marriage counseling when I received threats from your girlfriend who was your boyfriend. So I saw then the pain would remain. I failed to comprehend the extent of your love now because the love I gave in return is not enough and there was a constant need for someone else. Just keep someone else and I'll be not enough by myself. We argued about embarrassment. Why do I walk in front of you? Why am I always on the phone when we're in public?

Why am I embarrassed to be seen with you? I tell you, I like my private life PRIVATE and to you it was my excuse to cover being embarrassed of you. Little did you know I take ownership of what I do and I don't need anyone's permission for that. I own this. I can admit you were insecure about my being embarrassed of you, so I sent flowers and Edible Arrangements to your desk at work. I can admit I agreed to one a month date night so we can enjoy one another without the little ones. I admit that I would hug you from behind as we walked through the grocery store because these small gestures spoke to your insecurities. I never not admitted to our casual involvement and I never broadcasted it either. Now here it is further proving two things - I've never dated a woman, but I have been intimately involved with one. There's a difference. Women have to stop trying to force relationships on everyone they are sleeping with especially after it's been said I don't want a relationship or marriage. Embarrassed was how you tried to force a relationship and you later used it concerning marriage. I gave you more than you were ready for - you don't have to think I'm embarrassed of you - let's go get married today after work. Today never came. I have noticed in all this though to prove my love; I've had to be uncomfortable to prove I, so called, love you back. Who are you? What are you? How do you have this unique ability to make me question who I am though I appear to be so confident of who I am? Or is it merely the fact that I was wrong about me and you knew who I was the entire time? Tell me who you are! I don't want time to pass and we are here, right here in this moment yet again. I need these three times to be the only time I defy the saying, bitter and sweet can't flow from the same fountain. Because these three times I was able to love and to hate at the exact same time. I love you so much. I need you in my arms to remind me we are in this together.

I hate you so much that I could kill you and not bat an eye. I have a hatred strong enough to keep me from seeing you the same and a love so pure that I would never act on

my rage empowered by the hatred you bring
to me.

My Brokenness

"Abortion and racism are both symptoms of a fundamental human error. The error is thinking that when someone stands in the way of our wants, we can justify getting that person out of our lives. Abortion and racism stem from the same poisonous root, selfishness".

~ Alveda King

It Was Better to Have Killed Me

Why do you hate my existence?

Why am I the subject of your pain?

What is it about me that caused your life to change?

Why not listen to grandmother, abort the baby you don't want?

Why chose to look at me and feel tormented?

Why not give me away?

Why did you name me and bring me home?

Why did your mind not want me to stay?

Why not allow death to consume me?

Why did you continue to save my life?

Why keep me around to hate me?

Why do you believe this to be right?

Everyone that knows me, has knowledge that I am prolife. Though I do not believe abortion is right, I believe at times, that I should have been made an exception. There is so much that I would like to understand. I never wanted to have two kids because I never wanted a child of mine to experience my experience. They say parents have no favorites, but my life proves this to be untrue. My mother, at times, I feel has gone out of her way to reveal to me that my sister is her favorite child. It doesn't bother me that she the favorite, but Lord knows I hate feeling hated.

I thought that it was just me at first but then my son started asking questions. He wanted to know why our family not loves us. Why do they treat us differently? I asked him to explain and he said Meme treats me differently than my cousin. My sister and I both only have one child. He explained how when he and his cousin talks, she gets to go so much with Meme and when I am in town, everyone acts like I never came to visit. They never do stuff with me like they do with her. I asked him, did he feel as if he belonged to a family and he told me, yes, and named my friend's family. I then told him to be thankful to God that he was a part of a family even if they do not share a last name or bloodline.

I look over how things where and I really believe that, for that moment in time, my mother should not have allowed her Catholic views to have a part in her decision concerning abortion.

I should have been aborted and then she would not have so much of whatever it is that causes her to dislike me the way that she does. Even to dislike me to a point where while I was going through divorce and she could only say I told you not to marry him because something seemed off. You saw something off in him but didn't see the pain I had in losing the only man I ever loved because of a bad decision he made? And to dislike me enough to lie to everyone about my sexual preference? I have people contacting me because they say I know your mom haven't talked to you and I just want to know you're ok. I'm not a mommy's baby or a daddy's baby. She hates me and he's a rapist.

Now, what does this moment in my past have to do with the unfolding of situations and circumstances of my past? I found myself filtering my relationship with my sister through this funnel of brokenness. The things she said, the way she acted, and even down to something so simple as saying I love you, it filtered through a long funnel of distrust created by others. Because I already had trust issues from childhood, and unresolved issues that I had allowed to just be suppressed, her small mistakes exposed larger wounds.

When you forgive, you in no way change the past - but you sure do change the future.

~ Bernard Meltzer

Her expression of love was not rejected because it was not welcomed, but though it was longed for, the association with pain made it difficult to receive. I love her peanut head-self more than words could ever describe and she knows it. She's my rock and my friend, my prayer partner and my pick me up. She is my partner in crime and my co-pilot in traveling. God made no mistakes. Had I took matters into my own hand and had my way, I would have walked out on her at the first sight of controversy. I used to say friends don't argue, but my sister and I had to learn to communicate. This was not an easy task and we still mess it up at times. Surely what we had in mind and what GOD is doing with us is not the same. It is proof that our thoughts are not HIS thoughts and our ways are not HIS ways.

I know surely that, because of how much alike we are, and we like to stick to our saying, "My cut off game strong" when it comes to walking out on people, that we have both at one point or another in our relationship desired to walk out on one another when the going got a little tougher. We share being stubborn in common and we both have had life experiences where we have felt the need to be in control. But we had to acknowledge we have no control in this situation.

What makes THIS relationship special? What makes this experience different?

What makes this different?

Ladies, have you ever had a disagreement with a family member or friend? I'm sure we all have. Well, listen, I had a disagreement with my sister, Semaj that sent me to an unfamiliar place, normally I could have a disagreement with people and would just completely walk away or just cut off but this was different. As I allowed myself to walk away, I could hear God saying your normal routine is no longer acceptable in this assignment for I have equipped you for this. God began to expose me to little pieces of his plan as I would pray and fast. His pull on dealing with my sister became more required than I could have ever thought. I could hear God in my ear saying, you know what is required in this season; pray without ceasing for it is my desire that you stay close. Who will you obey, man, the enemy, or me? Said the Lord. I don't care how challenging it may get. Retreat and come back at my feet so I can prepare you in the spirit for what you will have to experience physically. I have equipped your hands for war and your finger for battle for you will be granted access to a place that no man has been able to get close to in this season. Stand up, put on the full armor of God, said the Lord, for LIFE is at hand. No matter how much you are rejected, cast down, or disregarded, dust your feet off and be still and know that I am God.

Do ya'll know how hard this is? I mean, I had to turn and ask God really this is what's you require from me? God are you sure? The Lord responded with John 15; I am the true vine, and my Father is the husbandman. Every branch in me that beareth not fruit he taketh away: and every branch that beareth fruit, he purgeth it, that it may bring forth more fruit. Now ye are clean through the word which I have spoken unto you.

Abide in me, and I in you. As the branch cannot bear fruit of itself, except it abide in the vine; no more can ye, except ye abide in me. I am the vine, ye are the branches: He that abideth in me, and I in him, the same bringeth forth much fruit: for without me ye can do nothing. If a man abide not in me, he is cast forth as a branch, and is withered; and men gather them, and cast them into the fire, and they are burned. If ye abide in me, and my words abide in you, ye shall ask what ye will, and it shall be done unto you. Herein is my Father glorified, that ye bear much fruit; so shall ye be my disciples. As the Father hath loved me, so have I loved you: continue ye in my love. If ye keep my commandments, ye shall abide in my love; even as I have kept my Father's commandments and abide in his love. These things have I spoken unto you, that my joy might remain in you, and that your joy might be full. This is my commandment, that ye love one another, as I have loved you.

Greater love hath no man than this, that a man lay down his life for his friends. Ye are my friends, if ye do whatsoever I command you. Henceforth I call you not servants; for the servant knoweth not what his lord doeth: but I have called you friends; for all things that I have heard of my Father I have made known unto you. Ye have not chosen me, but I have chosen you, and ordained you, that ye should go and bring forth fruit, and that your fruit should remain: that whatsoever ye shall ask of the Father in my name, he may give it you. These things I command you, that ye love one another.

If the world hates you, ye know that it hated me before it hated you. If ye were of the world, the world would love his own: but because ye are not of the world, but I have chosen you out of the world, therefore the world hateth you.

Remember the word that I said unto you, the servant is not greater than his lord. If they have persecuted me, they will also persecute you; if they have kept my saying, they will keep yours also. But all these things will they do unto you for my name's sake, because they know not him that sent me. If I had not come and spoken unto them, they had not had sin: but now they have no cloak for their sin. He that hateth me hateth my Father also. If I had not done among them the works which none other man did, they had not had sin: but now have they both seen and hated both me and my Father.

But this cometh to pass, that the word might be fulfilled that is written in their law, they hated me without a cause. But when the Comforter is come, whom I will send unto you from the Father, even the Spirit of truth, which proceedeth from the Father, he shall testify of me: And ye also shall bear witness, because ye have been with me from the beginning. Suddenly, I was reminded that my ways are not God's ways, and my thoughts are not God's thoughts. But God was requiring me to endure the affliction in his name's sake because he was about to perform good work in us both. Where he had called us, we didn't come ourselves, but the anointing of his power and the spirit of the Holy Ghost lead us here and it was up to us to allow God complete control despite how we feel or think. My God, you never really know how much control you truly have had on things until God calls you to a place of complete surrender and there is nothing you can do. People will try to talk you out of this assignment, but God will allow no such thing to shake. Come on, I know you have been hooked up with some people. Others may have not been too fun. Or maybe you have been that person others tried to declare people to leave you alone because of your current state or how you looked in you right now? What happens when God captivates your eyes to allow you to see the way he sees and you no longer see people for who they are but what they are destined to be? Because of brokenness, how do you show someone the love of God and help them look and believe past what they have been through; what their circumstances are, and what they think the situation should be? Love was the answer of God. With the fruit of the spirit I have equipped you to be quick to listen, slow to speak, and slow to anger is my requirement from you. So your sister can't hear, you be the ear, and because she can see, allow her to see but you God before that and reveal what the enemy has tried to hide. Ok GOD I SAY YES, DO I SPEAK Of THIS, HE SAID JUST LISTEN, HEAR MY VOICE, GIVE ONLY WHEN I SAY and WHAT I SAY. WHATEVER I am in will not fail. Remember, whatever I AM IN WILL NOT FAIL.

Touch her brokenness and remember what you make happen for others, I will make happen for you. People will wash their hands with you, but I declare you not to give up for I have prayed that your faith fail you not. Lynné, despite the failures you think you have experienced in life, has not my word been faithful to do my will?!What I desire for you both is to know this; what the enemy meant for evil, I'm turning around in this journey for your good. Joy, this is not just about your sister, but you will be revealed to your sister. All of the brokenness you have hidden from people and only she can see I designed it that way. Now go say this and she will know it is me. We both have the power to touch things and cause healing, but in this place, I will be required to lay hands on your brokenness, and you required to lay hands on my brokenness. No matter how far this has to go, seek God and listen, watch and Pray for highs and lows are required on this journey lean not on your own understanding but acknowledge me, says the Lord, and I will direct your path! Be mindful of your thoughts, Semaj, for she can hear them, and Joy, be mindful of your words because they have hurt her.

Be inspired by each other knowing that relationships are a gift from God. This will teach you that you can't commit to people before you commit to God. People can't fit gods place. So stay tune into God and connected build a prayer daily habit spend time in the word to help you become more sharpen worship in and out of the church environment. Keep these Five words near; Forgive, Pray, Serve, Sing, Love. You both serve a purpose, invest in this. It's not about quantity but quality. Protect and guard your friendship with balance and boundaries. Tap into your inner self and Rebuild, Reset, and Reconnect. It's necessary that you do that. At one point in attempting to filter through pain that we didn't give up on one another, I asked her to write and would give written responses. She wasn't a great communicator, and I have a passion for writing. I learned that sometimes it's easy to talk to yourself by putting your thoughts on paper. So, we wrote and while I can't share every detail and every writing, maybe this will give you a little look into our pain on paper.

Dear Big Sis,

I have been thinking on this and if I had to compare the uniqueness of who we are to a story, I came up with the Promise of Abraham. I chose this story because God sent a word to the earth with purpose attached. Profound purpose. I believe that, however, when God dispatched the promise, Satan dispatched peril. I truly believe that "Two are better than one, because they have a good return for their labor: If either of them falls down, one can help the other up. But pity anyone who falls and has no one to help them up. Also, if two lie down together, they will keep warm. But how can one keep warm alone? Though one may be overpowered, two can defend themselves. A cord of three strands is not quickly broken. But what happens when distraction comes for them at the SAME

TIME? How do they recover? So we are familiar with Abram receiving a word his descendants being blessed and he questioned God because he did not have children at the time. Then God promised him a child of his own when he was 75 years old, yet the promised child was birthed when he was 100. According to the parable, he went to his maidservant and conceived a child. This story shows the PROBLEM vs PROMISE. Within the text, Abram took matters into his own hands. He found himself slightly angered with the results, but it took 25 years for the promise to arrive from the time of the reveal. I don't have 25 years, 25 weeks, 25 days, 25 minutes, or 25 seconds to be outside of the place that God intended for me because I've taken matters into my own hands. The Songwriter said "tomorrow, I'll give my life tomorrow. I thought about today. But tomorrow very well might be too late". I need to make the effort to make it RIGHT TODAY! Starting with a blank apology for ALL offenses known and unknown, seen and unseen - in word, thought or deed. Forgive me. While I may not be deserving of forgiveness, I request it anyway. From something so small as you feeling I don't take time to understand you when you communicate to so large as you feel I "pop off" when upset. You are my sister and my friend; I love you and I'm grateful to have you/ your support.

Signed,

Returning Prodigal Daughter

Dear Sis,

Today I forgive you! Today I love you!
Today I ask that the words out of my mouth
and the meditation of my heart and your
heart be acceptable in God's sight. The
reveal of God's plan was we had to come
out of bondage, the release time was never
known, but deep down we knew something
unsettling was about to take place – we just
didn't know when or how. Sister the
question was how one can keep warm alone,
my answer is by the Holy Spirit. God has
the ability to wrap us up in his anointing
and keep us in a way that not even death
can shake us. I encourage you to get filled
up and keep pushing, even if you have to go
alone. Get a souled out spirit to serve GOD,
no matter what, and who is or is not there.
As long as you got JESUS, you don't need
anyone else! I thank my God every time I

remember you. You are my friend and I'm always in prayer for all my friendships and relationships through Christ. I always pray with joy because of your partnership in the gospel from the first day until now, being confident of this, that he who began a good work in you will carry it on to completion until the day of Christ Jesus. So, you say what happens when distractions come for them both at the same time? I'll tell you GOD happens. God's mercy and grace keeps and protects HIS children! GOD moves even before the enemy attacks. Because of his love for you and I, HE called my name. Just like in the Book of 1 Samuel, I heard his voice. I couldn't run or hide. I had to hear GOD's words and move quickly because death was trying to take place. In distraction, God has strengthened our hearts and ears to hear and obey. So, if you would allow as HE reveals more of the plan, have an open mind, ears, and eyes to see, to walk, and serve as we move from great to greater. Sister, our yesterdays are no more. Come on serve the Lord with me. Let's enter in his courts with thanksgiving, understanding this was GOD's perfect work in the most important time.

ALJ

How do we recover? We press toward the mark for the prize of the high calling of God in Christ Jesus, leave behind all things that are behind, and follow Christ. Without ceasing, we repent; we cry; we pray; we laugh; we dance; we worship; we be a friend in the time of trouble; and in good cheer, win victories. It is God who has redeemed us and we must get to work! So today, I tell you that you are not alone. God is with you. He has placed this friendship in our life with purpose. A relationship or friendship is a gift from God. Don't handle it the same way you would handle things unimportant, but nurture it, value it, protect it, respect it, because God has blessed us with it.

We know GOD is not done. We will be quick to listen, slow to speak, and slow to anger putting on the full armor of God and allowing him to guide us through this. We will continue to praise him in advance for how the impact has blessed us to fall at his feet and become humble and sincere. Understanding we may not be worthy of his grace; God sees us as worth it for the blood HE shed. All is well. It was good when we were afflicted. Greater is coming.

We will walk in the fruit of the spirit and when things come, we will speak GOD's word over the storm, not allowing flesh, emotions, or foolishness to taint what God is doing. I love you. We got this because we have God in His rightful place. Now let's be great!

Some may think my forbidden love is a testimony to the power of GOD. It is not. It's still a test. I know I will conquer this because in all things I'm more than a conqueror but I'm frustrated with GOD and myself.

With GOD

>how do you allow me to love forbiddingly?

With Myself

>how can you not be attracted to anyone else like this but one? >how did you stay when you saw it was unhealthy?

 >how do your dumb!@= still love someone that attempted to assassinate your character, tarnished your reputation, and brings nothing out of you that was a silent battle?

>how do you not know who you are?

You fought your own imaginations for years thinking you were supposed to be gay. Why did God allow you to be raped? Now that you crossed the line, where are you?

I fight me daily. It's worse than any battle Satan has, I feel. And it's harder because when I don't have answers, I feel disappointed and get disgusted with myself for falling for her. The whisper of suicide get loud but I don't believe in forgiveness from committing suicide. Ugh.

Fake Friends

What I thought was the perfect friendship caused me my deepest pain to date. Though it's been a year of what was assumed perfection, this road wasn't always the best one traveled. We have shared a few birthdays, holidays, and intimacies, this has been an uphill battle that was a long time coming for it falling apart. In the beginning things had a great start. It was all about the power of prayer and keeping one another encouraged. As women, we have to learn that we are not competing with one another. We should be one another's greatest assistance and I thought that I found that – loyalty for a change. It started with a dream, if it was a dream at all. There was a conversation between her and I where she asked me not to laugh or be offended. It was the beginning of our "transparency moments". I agreed not to laugh and asked that she be transparent, explaining that this would be our new code word – "transparent". You know that kind of word that opens the door for an amnesty. Her transparency moment was she dreamed the night before that she kissed me and it made her feel weird. I didn't think it was funny or anything but was curious as to what lead the dream on. I had questions. She explained that she had never been with a woman and neither had I. As the conversation continued, the subject was changed, a movie, some wine, and then that random off guard kiss was crazy, had prayer and went separate ways. It felt strange and not so strange at the same time. A few days later, I received a normal text, "What are you doing?" A few texts later, "I'm coming over." It was completely OK with me and that was the night that everything about who we were to one another changed. I became the prey. She came over to talk because things were a little awkward, but cordial. I was so confused. I remember crying, her hugging me, a gentle kiss, and the next morning I wake and there she still lies. It was my first time.

My Sister's Keeper

When I was invisible,

She saw me.

She listens for the voice of God,

He spoke and made me visible.

I cry because I was on his heart.

Mother told me love would heal,

But my brokenness didn't comprehend.

Joy, I was in search for,

But depression was my closest friend.

I cry because I wanted to be apart.

God knew I grieved,

Mom and sister never understood why
mine loving me not.

I knew that my vulnerability was hidden,

Sending friends to take family spots,

I cry because this is my fresh start.

There is a time to mourn and time to heal.

Joy is scary because of its unfamiliar feel.

Broken but not alone anymore,

Born to win my season's here,

I cry in awe of God's perfect art.

shEmotions

I can think back on so many occasions that I just felt like giving up and there was really never anyone to pull me through. Well, at least I always felt there was no one in my corner. Truth is I had experienced so much rejection from people that I wanted to love me that I was rejecting others that were willing to love me. I had entered into such a sunken place that the dark voids on the inside of me was consuming the light that attempted to shine on me.

Before I was able to accept my sister in Christ, I first rejected my spiritual mom. She was on assignment. She knew there was a dark place on the inside of me that only love can light up. I can't believe that I'm saying this, but I want to say that we went back and forth for nearly five years. She spoke life into me, prayed for me, loved on me, but in return, I ignored much of what she said, didn't trust her love, and had her placed in a box. For me, it was time wasted. She was consistent with breathing life into me, but I was hurt. I've heard "prophets" say I was lost in this season of my life. However, I wasn't. I was just broken. I was so concerned with self-preservation that healing was not even an option. Mother loved me, anyway. She loved me hard. She loved me consistently. She loved me by waring with the devil in prayer. She loved me through encouraging words. She loved me in such a way that love for me – the image of love for me was being returned to what GOD intended for love to be viewed as.

Don't misunderstand what I'm saying here. I'm not saying that my birth mother did not or does not love me. In my maturing, I have learned that the way she loves vs the way that I desire to be loved are not the same. Sometimes when we are loving others, if we are not speaking their love language, then our acts are in vain. There were things I needed according to my love language. But because I was not receiving them from the people around me, GOD provided. It was out of prayer that my spiritual mother was heaven sent to meet me at the place I was in and provide what I needed in a manner that would be noticeable to me.

See, mother provided something for me that was nothing less than what is biblical love. She was unconditional. Even in my place of sin, I heard from her saying I love you more than I am disappointed in you. Did I know she was disappointed concerning my drinking, occasional smoking, and having a same sex partner? Of course, I knew she was disappointed. The love that she provided gave me conviction and not a guilty conscious. Healing is not birthed from guilt. Her love was truly expressed, "There is therefore now no condemnation to them which are in Christ Jesus, who walk not after the flesh, but after the Spirit. For the law of the Spirit of life in Christ Jesus hath made me free from the law of sin and death".

Have you experienced someone that love you to a place that you fully comprehend that moment in the Bible when Jesus asked the crowd who was without sin among them? See, this love; this compassion; this empathy was new to me. Initially, I didn't trust it. However, when I saw the GOD in it, it made all the years to come after much easier. It made life a little better. It made maturing a little easier as well. Let's be honest, it made Vachelle a lot better in the totality of who she is - a better person, a better mother, and I would go so far as to say a better Christian. Yes, indeed, I am a better Vachelle.

Therapy Me

If you knew who I was, would you love me less?

If I released my secrets, could you handle what I confess?

If you find I don't live out the Bible, would you think I'm going to hell?

If you learned what I've done, could you still love Vachelle?

I know I'm not perfect and I don't try to be,

I know I'm brutally honest so don't lie to me.

I know I love too hard and I hate it about myself.

I know love gets me hurt and will be the death of me.

I'm tired of living in fear but I must protect myself,

I'm tired of people thinking I'm successful when I'm still learning wealth,

I'm tired of being judged for who I am and I don't know me,

I'm tired of making mistakes and N*ggas think they own me.

1.   I was raped by Dad, but you can call it relations

2.   Thought my ex-husband was in love, but found that he was faking

3.   I shut down on life because I wanted to die

4.   I could fathom leaving my son with pain in his eye

5.   I never dated a girl, but I let her f*ck me

6.   I don't ever want to be married; I fear that he won't love me

7.   I believe in God, but I struggle with healing

8.   I can't be cheating on pain, I get this guilty feeling

L oved ones want me to see a therapist but doctors also be crazy. See, if I go to the doctor, I have to this trauma phase me. I kinda like that she keeps talking about me - she likes me in her mouth. She is lucky it's not my pistol and her bloody couch. How can you continue to care for the people that burned you? It comes from giving my love vs making them earn me.

My first love was my father. This should be the testament of any girl but not in this aspect. He was literally my first love. I didn't even know that molestation/incest was wrong until years had gone by. When I learned how bad this actually was, for some time, I felt I was like the people of Sodom and Gomorrah. I was broken. Broken beyond brokenness. I found it hard to trust men because I trusted him, and he only used me for personal gain. Yes, I can say I felt used because I was 12 at the beginning and 17 when it ended. Though learning it was wrong, it never made me say I don't want to, because I was comfortable.

Then I exposed it all to Kris. He didn't judge me at all. In fact, he just loved me past the pain. Yet we were not even old enough to love or be in love. I had attachment issues and probably still do. His loyalty to me made me not want to lose him so I went above and beyond to make him know I was just as loyal to him. I'm loyal to those loyal to me. I married him. That loyalty went far. Too far. I didn't think that I would ever expose that I really didn't want to be married to him. Though I didn't want to marry him, I didn't want him to feel the pain that others had put me through. I was becoming numb to pain and my actions to protect others; it meant a lot of sacrificing self. We were young trying to be married the right way and he wasn't happy. He fell into the arm of another man. I didn't want to fall from the will of GOD and get divorced, so I tried to be married without sex. Things didn't go so well, and it meant we needed to part ways. December 2010 was the beginning of me shutting down. I feared love and had trust issues. I worked hard and allowed time to pass.

In 2018, I felt as if enough time had passed. I was tired of dreaming of loving and being loved yet not experiencing it in my reality. I wasn't searching but if I stumbled upon my secret desires, then to GOD be the glory. Accidentally, someone loved me the way I desired to be loved. They learned my love language and spoke to my mind, body, and soul. This was my forbidden love_ forbidden lover. Sad because here I am, 32 years old, and experiencing love for the very first time. I knew it would be short lived because the GOD in me would soon overwhelm this play in homosexuality. Side note - how did I go from homophobic to having a female lover?

Lynné spoke to me in ways I've never known I could communicate. She allowed me to cry without judging my weakness. So often people only see strength they forget I too am human. She knew when to hold me close and push me away. She mastered when to be my satisfaction and when to be quiet as my mood wasn't the best. She heard the loudness of my silence. She prayed - we prayed - but the sin of it all had me by the balls. I had moments that I pushed her away and made her feel as if she was not wanted/needed and in the same breath gave her feelings of being the most important thing to me after my kid.

I've probably been "in love" twice and, both times, it was frowned upon and against my very own religious beliefs. The first time I wasn't even old enough to consent or do anything more than be along for the ride. The second time, she gave me a high. But she definitely didn't walk away without giving me the lowest low I've ever experienced. Depression has nothing on the darkness she gave me.

During the high times, I remembered all that she said that she lacked and found a way to provide it. I cooked, I cleaned, I did the maintenance on the cars, and became the answers of relief, physically, than her dreams of store-bought toys could provide. She complained of never getting that relief from her children's fathers; so, that meant for me that I was studying her mental and her physical.

I was attracted to her brokenness and wanted to make it right. I wanted to expose her to the kind of people that she was not accustomed to. I had been so privileged in my upbringing to be exposed to something different. Growing up in Birmingham as a child, our "thugs" had a code that was honored. Children and women were off limits. If a drug dealer lost his mother, his rivalry looked out for him so that he could grieve then it was business as usual again. The military has shown me the ultimate form of loyalty. Soldiers don't really get to see color or anything else. There was a saying, look to your left and to your right. We are who we have, and it could be life or death.

Broken people respond to life from their brokenness. I wanted the best. My heart was in the right place and I went about it all wrong. I am different. I was exposed to different. I don't know what it's like to be aware of being cheated on in relationships by more than one person. I don't know what it's like to not feel loved or appreciated by the people I'm involved with. I mean, my boy Talley used to order me shoes he knew I would like just because he didn't need a reason and I loved when he told me he got a gift he had sent. Crenshaw was faithful with just popping up to cook in my kitchen. Cooking is his first love and he loves making people happy with what he loves. My friends are different, so I didn't relate to her tarnished ideal friendship and, or love.

How do I go from brokenness to brokenness at such alarming rates? What is it in me that brokenness finds me? This was no longer about how some "friend" of mine living in my house allowed someone to convince her to attempt to tarnish my reputation. Who gets paid to make friends look bad? This was about me and what GOD has on the inside of me. In order for me to be in this position, there is something on the inside of me that people need. There is something that I need to understand about me that I comprehend why others are envious of what's in me. What is it that God said about me that the enemy is fighting to a point where I am ready to end my own life? What is it in me that this person that "loves" me had her father threaten to kill me all in the name of being a pastor in Dallas? Something is in me.

There was something that I was promised. A friend of mind reminded me that, even though I was in pain, it was time to live out what God promised me. I had to go back to the words that had been spoken of me but had not yet come to pass. What did the prophet say concerning me? The prophet had spoken years ago that before I was formed in my mother's womb, I would be a healer. How can one heal if they have not experienced brokenness?

I needed a therapist…. **Therapy me!**

I Am My Own Frenemy

I n today's moment of reflection about who I am, what has molded me to become this way, and how I can get better - I find that I am my own frenemy. It's not about the person who hurt me; nor is it about the challenging experiences I have had - It's about me and the perspective I have had in this various instances. Giving unto others has been more about the lack that I have experienced and my feelings of inadequate help/support.

I loved extremely hard because I only wanted to hear/see the words 'I love you' without so many strings of need/ necessity attached to it. I've experienced so many "loves" out of the necessity of who I am and my limited talents that my response is not 'I love you too,' but what do you need from me. In this most recent season of my life those who have shown genuine love express it verbally and my response is thank you.

Healing is not about the volume of hurt experienced - but the minimal adjustments made to the essence of who you are.

Brokenness is a state of being that repeats when one does not take time to adequately heal. The weapon used to pain them is projected onto others without actually realizing you are hurting the ones that love you.

It's with my most recent experience of being hurt that my knowledge of healing deepens. When the situation replayed over and over in my head, the one thing that I started to see that wasn't there before is my very own incomplete healing. The things I thought before were all overturned by this "me" thoughts.

I was able to be broken by another person for two reasons -

    1.   I didn't notice, in the moment, the brokenness that was being projected because they, themselves, had not healed from all the different things that had broken them and were being stacked on each other. How does them not

healing have an adverse effect on me? It's their ability to relate to my unhealed areas of my life that makes me attractive to begin with.

2.   Personally, I don't know if it was the ideal of healing or the fear of having my flaws exposed that kept me from healing; so very nearly I have had these hidden wounds neatly places in the darkest shadows of who I am. They have been neatly tucked and carefully covered that they are not seen. However, it's the hidden energy that they possess that attracts energies alike.

My childhood still has a powerful hold over me. I had to think long and hard about these things that will come next and I decided to say them anyway. We are being transparent, right? For far too long, I have been hurting but more concerned with how others would perceive my hurt than doing what was necessary to heal. Enough is enough. It was in this buried hurt that my own wounds reopened, and I was projecting that hurt on others.

The worst feeling in the world is desiring to be accepted by someone that rejects you constantly. This is an everyday feeling. I want to let go but it consumes me. It gives me a hatred in my heart for my aunt's death. If my aunt was alive, there would be no doubt in my mind that someone loves me and accepts me for who I am today and who I am becoming tomorrow. I've experienced enough fake love for a lifetime. Too many people have found me to be disposable and serving temporary purpose for personal gain - probably money.

Lord, please don't allow my heart to be cold towards my son. I need for him to always feel wanted and knowing I am always in his corner. I want this because I know how the opposite feels very well. I'm so glad that I never had another child so that neither of them would feel in a competition for my love. My calls go unanswered most days and those simple hellos comes off as if I am a bother. I hate it here. Conversations feel forced and everyone wonders why I feel like such an imposition on them. I am the strongest person ever with more weaknesses than anyone can imagine. This life is depressing. I want too many to experience love in all the right ways. Someone that wants me for who I am and not money I don't have.

I Give Up!

So many claims to see so much concerning me and what God has in store for me. Meanwhile, I am literally struggling to take a breath daily. It has been amazing to help the few that I have come across along the way. For this, I am grateful. I have days where I barely see the need to get out of bed. I am worn out.

As far as playing with this lifestyle, I was unaware that I was. I am a perfect balance of 13 and 31 all at the same time. I was forced to mature while never growing up. I'm not running from anything; I'm hurting beyond self-preservation. I often see the opposite of what everyone else sees and it's surreal.

You See	I See
Married	Bitter/Broken
Gifted	Misunderstood
Talented	Self-taught trade
Half Full	Half Empty
	Church Hurt
	Resentment
	Depressed
	Sad
	Unaccomplished

I have just felt confused about what's next and no one in my corner (no disrespect to anyone who feel they have been supporting me). Why am I abandoned/orphaned at thirty-one? What made me not worthy of being loved too? Why is there a favorite? My issues came long before I ever got entangled with a woman. I was yearning for a healthy relationship for a long time.

I know he feels like my feeling are exaggerated, but I know my sister is the favorite and I don't care. I just don't want to feel as if I have to do something drastic to hear I'm proud of you or be noticed. Thank God for my Godmother because I have been able to express these feelings of being unwanted for decades. I have even asked her, if I had to feel this alone why not have just aborted me? I've asked how long will I be a disappointment for my teen pregnancy? What will I ever do to be good enough? I gave up.

I love and support others, but I feel like 97% of the time I have nothing to show for it. Loving hard has given a lifetime of heartache and just want "something" to fill the void. My aunt is gone so nothing is there. So yes, I let her temporarily "complete" me because she heard me; she says me. She says the tears I never cried. She heard the pain in my voice that was invisible to so many others. It was mutual. I saw her. I heard her.

I won't call myself depressed. What adjective do you use to describe my loss of interest, weight gain, trouble sleeping, feeling worthless [unaccomplished/failure] and trying to cry myself to sleep? I honestly wish I was never hurt or brokenhearted trying to love again through my tainted views of love. I wish I could just get over it. I can't. I want to but I'm stuck.

I want to love my second husband without fear of him taking everything I have worked to rebuild. I mean the first husband left with it all with no input to what I had gained. Screams what have I rebuilt? I don't think I have seen more than $10,000 in my savings since my ex stole this kind of money from me. I was bound to own a home at twenty-one; so, how did I end up temporarily living out of my car at twenty-nine? I feel like I've lost my first love.

My aunt was my sense of peace to confide in, hold my hand, listen to me, and encourage me. But August 17, 2006, left my life permanently changed. Now I'm trying to be this to myself. I'm in pain and living with this high intense pain is who I've become. Take the pain away, and who am I?

I am Toxic

T hat happens when you compartmentalize hurt, but never take the time to heal? You think you know what's good but you are just covering wounds and hiding them. Improperly healed wounds become infections and untreated infection is toxic. I am just that. I am that toxic that came from a wound that was covered and another wound and then another and there is no healing. People looking to you for healing but you, yourself, have not healed at all. I am that toxic. My toxicity doesn't know right from left but masked in love. Is my love toxic? I have given half my love in many relationships. My ways became manipulative and characterized under self-preservation.

It was October 8, 2018, when she said to me, "If she prays for you, looking out for you, you're on a whole other level." This statement had so much purity when it was made and things should have remained in this place. The worse thing for two individuals that are big on the things of God can do is to partner with someone like them in the sense that we were both broken and not seeking healing just masking the hurt in helping others. Light years happened in a few moments, it seems. I have been a guarded individual for a long time, but I wanted to change. On October 16, 2018, that morning, she just simply said I'm proud of you for allowing me in even when you don't understand why. I felt it was an answer to my prayers to simply feel loved and feel safe. I expressed this and made a promise to be transparent in my emotion which I often don't do. I will acknowledge that being transparent is not for everyone.

When you release things into the atmosphere, it's almost like you have given the devil permission to attack you. My confession on this day was I really wish I were a boy; life would be so much easier as a boy. She heard me and encouraged me with these words, "I think it's just because you are finally at a place where you are allowing yourself to have emotions and it's all over the place, you will get to a place where it won't

VACHELLE S. JEMISON

be as hard and I'll be your sister and that's it.
Right now your feelings and emotions are all
over – just trust the process and trust God."

Who would have ever thought that by
October 17, 2018 she would have possession
of me? I have no words, yet I have no
regrets either. Yes! Even after being hurt by
the lies told, I can still say I love this person.
I don't believe that love fades with offense -
that's not love, its lust or infatuation.

Faithful are the wounds of a friend;
profuse are the kisses of an enemy. From my
current view looking over this I can't even
tell you if this is the wound of a friend or the
kiss of an enemy. I do, however, have one
word…. PAINFUL.

I am not mad nor can I any longer be
upset because I am my own level of toxic. I
can say that I feel offended; I will
acknowledge a sense of betrayal felt above all
these things because I, myself, having
unhealed wounds or improperly healed
wounds, was toxic to her brokenness. She

trusted me. She actually entrusted me with who she is, her secrets, her tears, and her heart. Just as I feel that I was broken; I cannot fail to consider the breaking that I have done in the process. I am harsh with words. Nice nasty if you will. Don't come for me and I won't hurt you for the sake of protecting me.

I can think of a time that speaks volumes to the lack of respect, love, and concern shown for her and her brokenness. I was excited about having a birthday and she went above and beyond to ensure I had a good time. I felt that no one had celebrated me before. Couldn't recall ever having a birthday party. I expressed how my feeling were hurt by this in the past, but in my old age, I had learned to accept that no one loved me enough to celebrate my life often using Thanksgiving being so close as an excuse. I mean she went above and beyond. Breakfast in bed, bubble bath, cleaned the house for me, took me to a trampoline park [I'm a kid at heart], got me tickets to see Creed II, and even set up a little small get together. She also surprised me with a cake and all. While at

the movie theater, we got into a disagreement
- and by 'we' I mean her because I don't really
argue. I sat on a banister and just asked if she
was done bitching and nagging. She was
offended by things I said rather calmly but I
knew it would hurt before I said them. I just
looked and simply thanked her for
attempting to ruin my birthday. She cried but
we went and saw the movie anyway. After
much time with the silent treatment from me,
I eventually apologized for intentionally
hurting her feelings after she was only trying
to express something that she was offended
by. I don't even remember what had her in
her feelings to being with. I just remember
being so condescending and cold. We went
back to the house and she was still upset,
packed all of her things and the kids' things
and ran for the door. My cousin convinced
her to stay. We later went to Top Golf, but I
was so upset that I felt she tried to make my
birthday about her, I just ignored her while
we were there. We got home that night and
she again packed to leave. I wasn't moved at
all. It was late, she had been drinking and I

refused to let her leave with the kids because she had been drinking. It was this night that I realized I had never experienced life before this night. Something changed. She was lying next to me and apologized for ruining my birthday. She explained that she actually wanted to make it the most memorable but not negative like that. She expressed her love and then she really expressed her love. It was that night, at thirty-two years old, that I truly experienced sex. It wasn't a competition. I had nothing to prove to her or to myself. I wasn't trying to convince myself that I could enjoy sex after being raped and that I was in control of my body. These are all the things that I dealt with in my head so many times before. I mean before her I tried to convince myself I wasn't into women. In that moment, a mix of emotions rushed through me. I had been afraid to be with a man because of my past traumas. I also feared being condemned by both family and church for being gay. I am woman and I enjoy her, but I could never date women. Not only did she pull emotion out of me, but she taught me to please this night. It was with her action this night that I gained clarity to Lil Wayne when he said you give brain so good I could have sworn you went to college - knowledge. It wasn't just that, but she introduced me to pleasing another's body and not just going through the motions. What a wonderful two or three hours. I was nose open but had to keep my cool.

I can see my toxic because it was unnecessary to hurt her feelings just because I could, and this would be the first of many times that I did this to simply "maintain control" of our situation. I often told her, we are not in a relationship because I don't do commitment, but just know that I'm only having sex with you. There were certain things I did to keep her at a distance for the sake of self-preservation that when I think of it now, I wonder if my behavior was narcissistic in nature. The charm, feeding off her compliments of how well I loved her, lack of empathy towards hurting her even when she expressed the hurt, her feelings, my words picked at her shortcomings at times, and if there is any sign that makes me question my actions was the constant dancing around defining the relationship.

Man, this woman went out of her way to love on me daily. She told me annoyingly too many times per day that she loved me. Small things to make me know in her own way- my favorite candy, watching things. I love that she hates, and when I looked at a pair of Jordan's with desire for too long, she would let me walk away and get them anyway. Each shoe box had a sticky note saying never question my love or gave me a specific reason as to why she loved me so deeply. I was more concerned with how others viewed our experience than living in the moment most of the time. My religious beliefs convicted me at times and I even tried pushing them to the side. At some point my confidence grew and I was comfortable just living in the moment. We went to her favorite places, dined at her favorite places, though she hated tennis shoes and I just loved them she embraced my world for me. In return, I even watched the dumb Love & Hip-Hop shows. I was comfortable and loving every moment of the sin I was in, but I was toxic.

I was so toxic that when she confessed that she was in love with me and could marry me – my initial response, I kept it to myself that I didn't hurt her feelings. Then I constantly questioned her and her thoughts to see if she would back down and change her mind. I knew it would be a cold day in hell before I married her, but I love this woman. I don't want to hurt her like before. I put a ring on it and called her bluff. I asked her to go marry me one day on a lunch break and told her I could understand it she was uncertain. To make things more favorable to me, I told her she had to be the one to tell our kids that we had run off and got married if she agreed. It was at this moment that she was ok with simply wearing a ring as long as I was ok with not denying her. This, for me, is simple because if you ask me no questions, I tell you no lies at all. I wasn't denying her; I was simply not volunteering the information of our entanglement.

This behavior was toxic.

What was it that had me so toxic that manipulation was a fall guy for me? Let's think about this. I don't want to marry you to a point where I position you to tell me no. This is crazy. LOL. Funny but not that funny at all. This is another person. This is their feelings. This is their life. In that moment, none of these things meant anything to me. I was the only one that mattered. I wasn't trying to be married and that to me mattered. It's one thing to play around with sin, but to go this far against GOD, you have to be a different type of stupid. I am not that kind of stupid or bold.

In the event that you are reading this, I was wrong. I apologize from the bottom of my heart. Hurt people hurt people. Unfortunately for us, we were two hurt people pretending not to be hurting trying to love one another. Love and self-sacrifice, we were accustomed to. When things became great and we were living together, enjoying our lives together with date nights and family time, me taking care of you because it made me feel good - and you taking care of me because you said it made you feel; I knew you love me- the doors opened for self-sabotage. I can look at this two ways, you self-sabotaged out of the fear of being happy for once or that way of escape that I closed the door on ones before I reopened in a way that I would return to the Father and things simply be a test to build me for my purpose. Either way, thank you.

Now I don't want to be that person that offers that generic apology because I was wrong. I was wrong for blowing off you telling me you had a dream that you kissed me. I was wrong for not speaking up when you actually kissed me. It had nothing to do with you entirely. I allowed this moment to unlock something that I knew was already there. Years ago. I questioned if I could tolerate this behavior and finally there was a chance to "test the waters" with no room for judgement for me. You know the people I know. You have never really left Oak Cliff, I had nothing to worry about concerning how people that knew me saw me. I was protected to an extent. Even when you tried to expose me, it wasn't enough. I was protected in this. I knew that I was protected, and this was the beginning of me taking advantage of this opportunity.

I apologize. You deserved more and you deserve better. This went from being a productive partnership as prayer partners to an experiment for me. This experiment got you paid to "expose" me out of your own hurt and to hurt me in ways that I wasn't aware that I could be hurt.

You deserved me being better at being myself. When your dad threated to kill me that was my way of escape to remove you from a relationship that was going toxic. I didn't let it go. I was more intrigued that this man had the unmitigated gall to threaten me and not know me. You thought it was well because I don't know him. He was actually quite easy to find. I knew what he looked like and wanted to see how far these people would really go.

This became the perfect example of not blaming the devil for the things that were to come. Yes! The Bible tells us, oh how they increase that troubled me and many are they that rise up against me. This wasn't the devil that these people were rising against me. THIS WAS ME. When God offered me a way of escape, and I took a seat at the table to have a plate of the destruction that was being prepared before me, this was my doing. I have to take full responsibility for my hand in this because prior training prepared me for moments just as these. But I am still the one that made a conscious decision to see the wrong and participate anyway. My ego was getting the best of me. I had failed to bring myself into submission to the way of God.

This was necessary.

You were necessary!

Moving On

Y ou can't move on from them until you stop moving back in moving back into what they did, moving back into talking about them, moving back into trying to make people think "you're good" by retelling the story. Listen, you're delivered, but you're not healed when you keep moving back in with thoughts and talk about the past. When tempted to move back in, when that look back spirit that Lot's wife had tries to suck you back in, remind yourself why God moved you out and tell the devil, "I was not defeated, I was delivered for my greater." This is your redo... old things have passed away; behold, all things have become new!

See, what can be understood from this trouble of mine is my suicide was not about me killing myself though the thought did cross my mind a time or two. Let me be transparent, I don't have it all together. I just make being stressed out look very well. I remember when I was first told this person that swore I was her best friend was paid to speak ill of me. Paid to use what I told you in confidence against me. Not many knew that I was told I have PTSD. However, she actually told others for the purpose of attempting to ruin me. Paid to say I tried to kill her and she was afraid of me. Can you fathom how this made me feel?

Kill you? Wow! I was overwhelmed. I thought I was about to lose it all. All that I had worked for. All that I had been through to make life better for my son, jealousy and envy was knocking at the front door. I refused to take an L this huge from someone that was only upset that I was honest about not wanting to be married to her.

Not wanting to commit had no bearing on my feelings. Nowhere should it have had one to doubt it. I was honest when I said I loved you. I just refused to be controlled by these small tactics of manipulation.

I was being overwhelmed with the thought of how much damage I could have possibly done to my son and his future because I chose to actively participate in a sinful lifestyle for a few months. I wasn't going to let him suffer like that. It was in this moment that it crossed my mind that taking my life would secure his. I had a made up mind and set a date. I was ok with her ruing my life but not my son's life. What kind of love was this that she had given me?

Had given my son?

I woke up early on a Saturday morning and loaded my weapon. I drove away because I didn't want my baby to be the one to find me. After I got to the parking lot of the bank that wasn't open. I just needed to say this one last prayer. As was sitting in the parking lot, my car read an incoming text from my son. "Hey Mom, I love you. I don't know where I would be without you or what I would do if you were not here". Ok, God what are you saying to me, do you not know my life is about to fall apart?

Well, I just drove home and cried the entire trip. Guess something wasn't right in the "spirit" because Sinamen called to make sure I was ok and so did my Mother. I cried a little more. Monday rolled around and I learned from the manager at my workplace that I was not being fired. He then told me that instead, they have done research on how to work with veterans with PTSD and wanted to meet with me to discuss potential accommodations that would help me.

The funny thing is I was relieved. My manager told me that there was nothing to be alarmed about that they were not concerned about her accusations. They had actually been watching her behavior for some time and was concerned about how she purchased my lunch nearly every day to a point of interrupting meetings I was attending to see if I was hungry, and suddenly to change to, "I was trying to kill her?"

Be careful when you decide not to walk away from certain people when God gives you the opportunity to, for the sake of your own loyalty or not wanting to hurt them. They, in turn, hurt you. This was my experience with Judas. To learn that someone was paid to attempt to destroy you. Jesus, how are you so good? How? How did you love Judas while knowing that he would do this kind of damage to you? How did you not lose focus on purpose? See, the human in me wanted revenge. The part of me that believes that God knows best only found peace. Peace in the fact that HE protected me even while I slept with my own enemies.

I didn't die that day from feeling overwhelmed. Anger had me gripped for months after feeling so betrayed. I had so much running through my head. I invited you into my home; helped with things you couldn't afford to do; responded to the grief of not being able to feed yourself during the holidays or purchase things for your children; my mechanic doesn't even know you, yet he only knows your car because mine is new. I was going broke mentally, emotionally, spiritually, and starting to sink financially.

Thank God for moving on. Moving on means die. I have been crucified with Christ and I no longer live, but Christ lives in me. The life I live in the body, I live by faith in the Son of God, who loved me and gave. I had to call in some reinforcement to get back to the place that sin almost took me away from. Let not sin therefore reign in your mortal body, to make you obey its passions. It meant I had to die a little more. Not only did I have to die, it meant I had to kill. Put to death therefore what is earthly in you: sexual immorality, impurity, passion, evil desire, and covetousness, which is idolatry. I had to kill things in me that were interfering with me living out purpose. I needed to remove the desire for revenge and take on peace that surpasses all understanding. I had to kill forgiveness and take a step back on God's love. I had to return to the basics. I needed to return to the warrior that I decided I no longer wanted to be. I had to go back to the fighter that I wanted to die.

See now? A warrior knows that she must be dressed for battle.

I had to overcome depression and put on the full armor of God that I might be able to fight the battle that was set before me. I lost focus when I only saw the face of the person and not the warfare that was present. If you know that you wrestle not with flesh and blood, then you can't look at the person who is being used to attack you. If we are honest, the person never would have been able to attack you had you not allowed them to get close to you. When the enemy attacks, it's strategic and slow. You want to attack an empire? Insert an insurgent. The purpose of this person is to gain your trust as well as insight on how you are running your empire.

I let my guard down. I was aware that there was an issue and gave that good old "benefit of the doubt". I am loyal to a fault and allowed this ideal of loyalty to be blinding to the reality of what I was experiencing. Moving on requires admitting you were wrong. Moving on requires a mind ready to repent. Moving on requires a heart of submission to the things of God. Moving on requires discipline. Just as I went to military combat training and had refreshers along the way, I had to bring some others in for the purpose of making sure I got the necessary refreshers. I needed to be restored.

Father God in Heaven,

There is someone that is reading this that relates. They completely understand this feeling of betrayal from a loved one. They are hurt. They are angry. They want answers as to why? They are looking for where they failed themselves as they go through the process. Father, thank you. Thank you that up to this point, they have not acted irrationally. Thank you they have not succumbed to the thoughts of revenge. Thank you for the realization that to act on revenge reveals a condition of the heart that they have and not the person that has betrayed them. Thank you that they are healing. Thank you that they are yielding to the voice of the Holy Spirit though it's a lot harder than it seems.

Lord humble us that we might step back to be properly clothed. I take the helmet of salvation and the sword of the Spirit, which is the word of God. Give me strength that I pray in the Spirit on all occasions with all kinds of prayers and requests. With this in mind, be alert and always keep on praying for all the Lord's people. Center me with God minded individuals that will pray also for me, that whenever I speak, words may be given me so that I will fearlessly make known the mystery of the gospel, for which I am an ambassador in chains. Pray that I may declare it fearlessly, as I should.

I am here before you as humble as I can be, broken hearted, hurt feelings, traumatized, and submitting myself in full that I do not stray away from the prose of God that is on my life. While it may seem difficult, here I am LORD surrendering all that I am daily. Even when I fall short, I surrender again and I will continue surrendering until I am made perfect by you.

I incline my ear to hear that your voice is louder than my troubles. You see this pain God and I am casting it upon you because you care for me. I don't want to stay in this place of pain, but if this cup is mine to bear, strengthen me *that I might not be overwhelmed by it. Cloth me, Lord, as only you can prepare me for whatever better belongs to me. He put on righteousness as his breastplate, and the helmet of salvation on his head; he put on the garments of vengeance and wrapped himself in zeal as in a cloak. According to what they have done, so will he repay wrath to his enemies and retribution to his foes; he will repay the islands their due. In Jesus name- AMEN.*

Confessional

Well Mom, I know nothing catches you by surprise and I chose for us to have this much need conversation though the confessional because I can't bear to see the look of disappointment on your face with some of the things that I deal with on my day to day. Over a six to eight-month time period, my thoughts have been haunted by my mistake and it has opened so many avenues for me to overthink many things in my head. For the most part, I have always been able to be completely honest with you concerning many things. There are some things that I chose to spare the details on, but the details are eating away at me inside.

I was excited to tell you about my "friend" because I felt that I had finally received an answer to my prayers. And I'm not saying that it was not an answer to prayer, I believe that I underestimated the sender of the answer. Everything sent is not from GOD and all bad things experiences are not an attack of the devil. Well, this experience has left me broken in two. I am emotionally torn between healing and being guarded as I fear to trust another because of her actions.

It replays in my head as to what I did or did not do that could have prevented this entire lost space that I am experiencing. That faithful October day when I thought it was nothing but a casual conversation - she had the dream that she kissed me, so she kissed me. She dreamed it was going further and it went further. Though this is my experience, what caused me to be paralyzed and even experience this? Why did I not move when it seemed there was an opportunity to escape? Did I stay too long? Did I fall too hard into sin? Why does this still haunt me after time has passed? I let go of a few friends as a response to her insecurities and now I am not even comfortable to go to my friends and say I messed up and this is what happened.

So here we are. First, please allow me to apologize for any undue stress, prayers, or anxiety concerning me. Far too many times, I make decisions such as this because of the excitement in the heat of the moment and nothing more. While I know the decisions were erratic, the temporary gratification was amazing and almost worth the headache. She had a dream that she would kiss me and I just thought it was funny. I took it lightly when she told me that God showed her that we would talk to one another. It fell on deaf ears. I didn't even tell you because I just thought to myself, she's tripping; neither of us are gay [well, I can only speak for myself]; and she would never be crazy enough to act on those dreams. One kiss lead to two kisses that lead into her later showing me she was certified in underwater basket weaving.

It touched places that I only dreamed, and it would one day come again. I had never explored sex for pleasure because I just never had interest. Was it the molestation that kept me from being interested or was it the unsettling feeling of not feeling good enough because my husband had a boyfriend? Well, whatever it was, she taught me to be open with some amazing talents and tactics. I don't know if it was the asking me to lunch part, or making me feel great in the car. Or was it the sweet messages that made me feel special throughout the day? Was it chocolate and Pepsi left of my desk at work nearly every day? Or, going out of her way to bring me a Faygo Redpop? Her being around was never about sex, but it was about intimacy. I spent so much time masking weaknesses with strength that it just felt good for someone to give me permission to be weak. I needed every moment of it. Those moments where I could lay on her back at night and cry because I felt my world was caving in; the moments she held me close because she knew something was wrong but I had no words; the moments I wanted to commit suicide and not being able to tell anyone what was eating me up inside.

It was not like the she didn't reap the benefits of having me around. The cooking, the cleaning and the handling of business because that's who I am. The edible arrangements, the flowers on the desk at work, the wanting to be like me so now Ms. 'I don't wear sneakers' was now quick to build outfits around the Jordan's that matched mine. The affirmations of why you might be a good person or the why you are beautiful messages because of thinking she is not pretty without make up. It made me feel good to hear that I was the emotional support that you wanted, especially after your sister reminded you that you were only cousins and didn't have your own parents. I can't imagine how that hurt, I wanted to be there. I needed to be there. I was there.

She was my rock. While I am generous to others more than I get it back, she was the one that gave it back. While it was only for a few months that we played this game, I enjoyed going to work and my favorite candies/soda was on my desk with a sticky note, 'I love you.' I appreciated finding lunch on my desk after a meeting when God knows I was too tired or frustrated to eat. The things that I had been doing for others to show appreciation for them being a part of my life, she did for me and it made it easy to give to her in return. I needed to list to her wants and her needs and give that and then some.

She was me and I appreciate her for who she is. Though things went left and she did what some might consider to be unforgiveable - I forgave and I still love her because love has no conditions. I can't just love you when you are right. Things slowly transitioned and the one or two nights a week we stayed together turned into her moving in. The family vibes that I had being praying for had come just not the way that I asked for them. We cooked together, prayed together, game nights, movie nights, and to make her remember, she was an adult we had grown folk's time.

It all seemed perfect and the kids loved it but we were unhappy with one another. The more we enjoyed the company, the more in my quiet time I said God, whatever is wrong make it right and all things out of order set them in order. Remove everything that is not like you from my life that you are able to get the glory from all I do. We agreed that we were in over our heads and needed some time apart.

I decided to treat her to hair and nails because I felt that though it was mutual to stop being intimate; my initiation of it caused pain and I didn't want to be associated to pain for her. At the salon, she was listening to others talk about how outside of God's will same sex relations are and the conversation was heated. BOOM. She had a moment and came rushing home to tell me about this time at the shop. She drew the conclusion that love is love and she was in love with me and she should enjoy that. Even if it did not last, she just wanted to enjoy the moment because I made her happy.

I love when love is not one sided because I knew she was in love but she was embarrassed because it went against what we believe as Christians. I am the opposite. I live in the moment, take responsibility for my actions, and enjoy the moment no matter where it stands. In this case, I had a made up mind to enjoy her and I was going to live with no regret. She was going to know she was loved in a way that spoke to her. I wanted to know her love language and speak to it. Gifts - she got those. Words of affirmation were too easy coming from me. The little girl in me that never learned to be good in bed because that part of my life stopped with molestation - she breathed life into it. She turned me into the freak everyone assumed I was. Backseats, parks, and parking lots and she really messed my head up the night she gave me a massage, a bubble bath, and performed oral underwater while I soaked in the tub. She literally sucked my soul out of me. It was this night that I knew that she would do whatever to be sure I was happy and that sense of happiness almost got a marriage commitment out of me. I knew that she was upset at one point that I disagreed so I turned the tables telling her one day we could leave work on lunch and go get married if I wasn't scared. She would show me exactly how much she loves me. I knew she would never go for that, and it definitely stopped her from questioning if I was embarrassed to be with her.

It's so crazy how sin will take you on a rollercoaster ride. The marriage I said I never wanted, the family life I thought I could never have, the companionship that was desired knowing that I just wanted to be around someone I could be unapologetically me - she gave me that person and I wonder if it was real. I was in love for the very first time in my thirty something years of existence. We even had this saying we said to one another nearly daily- Our love is forever. Always has been. Always will be. This was really no regret. If we crossed paths and I said 'Our love is forever,' and got no response, I will completely respect the lack of forgiveness for whatever she might feel I have done to offend her.

Now here we are, months later and it's yet another Thursday and something doesn't sit well with me. The Army taught me that attention to detail was everything. "Stay alert; stay alive". I noticed her moving things out slowly and I did not mumble a word. I felt if she wanted me to know she would communicate our problem. I'm praying about some things because the small sighs are very loud.

Then I get sick. Stomach twisting in knots and I was in so much pain, I was barely walking. We argued about going to the ER and then she disappeared to take phone calls. This was abnormal because we took calls on Bluetooth {we were open and honest so I thought}. A few phones calls, a little cuddling, and a great deal of secrecy led to me being awakened from my sleep to the sound of moving furniture. Movers came and were looking to remove things that were mine. I said nothing. Oh but when Monday comes.

So now it's Monday and I had a great

weekend of fun with my son and his girlfriend to see my boss at work two or three hours early. This bitch had the unmitigated gall to tell the people at work that I have PTSD and threatened to kill her. While I was extremely upset initially and almost wanted revenge, I was so mad, it was the answer to my prayer in the worst way.

Can I wonder from a moment? Was this real? Was this on purpose? Absolutely, because I had been warned by a third party that she was only looking to take advantage of me. I took her side because she laid next to me every night. The signs were there that the situation was toxic. A major sign was that she felt I hurt her before and her father called me and threatened to kill me. That was a major sign, but I forgave.

Hurt people, hurt people. Sadly, if hurt is not dealt with, people tend to self-sabotage situations as a defense mechanism. How in the hell did the person that text me I love you every day, several times a day; the one that called late at night saying I can't sleep without you, the one that had me so open and infatuated that when she said I can't sleep without you I got in the car and drove fifty minutes so she wouldn't have to.

Now I'm haunted in my head by this. Like literally haunted.

My Christianity is on the line, haunted by this.

1.   She left me desiring to love based on chemistry with no regard to gender

2.   I spent months struggling to pray because I was hurt that she lied on me

3.   As things replay in my head at times I question if she prayed for me or preyed on me

4.   Am I broken or angry because I don't know at this point?

The residue that remains is the soul ties that can be formed biologically, physically, emotionally, spiritually, and mentally. Strong soul ties are forged out of shared experiences and emotions. We shared being raped; being married; being divorced and feeling abandoned by loved ones. The strongest of them all is that the one person we felt we had in the world for love and support we had buried. She was my trauma bond that became my lover.

While this is the situation that unleashed so many things I will acknowledge that I wasn't healed. I was still mad at my father for molesting me and creating the engraved thought that I wasn't worthy of love. I was still upset with my ex-husband for cheating on me in a same sex relationship making me feel that I was incapable of loving a man the way that he deserved. I was still mad at my aunt for giving up on life [she didn't; she just died]. I was still mad at the fact that my family still punishes me, sixteen years later, for having a child at a young age as if it was their lives that were altered in some shape, form, or fashion. I was mad. I have these boxes of hurt that I have just sat to the side, because why should I be healed? Why should I tell my feelings? No one cares about me. People only care about what I have to offer and I was tired of offering a table of feast and getting the crumbs from the table I set.

Remember the song from the show Empire where he was trying to explain to himself that he was good enough? Remember he said,

"I gave you all of me

But it still ain't enough to make you happy

I gave you everything

It still doesn't measure up, no

It feels like I walked 5 thousand miles

And didn't even come close

Feels like I try to make you smile

But you don't even care, no"

I wasn't good enough for the people that I cared about most. For years, I felt like I was trying to force relationships and forced others to love and accept me. Sadly enough, I was trying to get family to accept me without even requiring that they respect me. I am a first-born stepchild. Like what the hell! I just want to be loved. I have been clear about not having a girlfriend but a female sex partner. Why did I have her though? She filled a void, but even more so was this an attempt at being rebellious as an adult? I have been chasing love a long time. Initially it was a tattoo at fifteen. Then it was going to the Army at seventeen because no one agreed with me. Since my aunt Samantha died, I've felt that I could not even purchase love and support from my own family. Reading my Facebook statuses and relaying them to others as if we have had conversations. Suicide was easy because I was already dead to the people that mattered most to me.

I was dead inside.

I was hopeless.

I was lost.

I was hurt.

This is me broken. And I have been broken so long that healing was not an option. I had just learned to hide being hurt and live with not being accepted. Not being accepted was such a big thing that I projected that onto others that wanted to be a part of my life. I was shutting people out and not giving them a chance to love me the way that I had hoped I could be loved. After she taught me how to be "ate", I let her eat away at my pain hoping that it would make me feel better.

I've talked to a therapist; I live an isolated life; and I'm out of ideas on how to be restored as I feel I lost my anointing with this mistake. It took a while to dream again and struggle to pray for others. I love good worship, but I struggle to talk to God because there is something that was awakened in this experience.

Attraction has no gender, just chemistry. I've fallen and lost hope in restoration. I have so many days where I can hear so clearly that death is the only way. I just don't believe in suicide, yet I struggle with the thought of it. I just want it to all be over. I want to have moments of rest by just sitting with you, mom, being hugged, and being loved on. How do I ever recover from this? Mom, I need help finding restoration as depression is consuming me. I failed you when I slept with her and I failed the gifts that God entrusted me with by choosing sin over and over. Is this what the prodigal son felt like? She was supposed to love me. She said she was in love with me.

She betrayed me.

I forgive her.

I forgive me.

A Mother's Love

This is like nothing I've ever written.
It's like nothing I've ever seen.
I'm so out of my element!
Lord, this must be a bad dream?
The first time I read the confessional,
It was chilling yet I was numb.
I had to pull myself together and
 remember
I am the mom!
Hit by this bombshell
Thinking,
Lord am I equipped?
Head spinning out of control with the
thought of you ladies playing with each
 other's drip!
This little Entanglement, as you call it,
 I must admit... not totally surprised. It
had you losing control, almost led to your
demise.
Oh what drama! But at the core of this
mess lies unresolved childhood trauma.
Lord-------Lord, I pray for my children! I
even turn down my plate.

Jesus, I ain't equipped for THIS but I need
you to clean my child's slate! God, I fear for
her life, I fear for her soul!
Please, God, show me my role!
What's my reason in this season?
This child has gone all the way left.
What she's done goes against what I
believe...
Lord, I need your help!
    Father, my ears are wide open, my is
heart focused on things above

As I sit and wait for answers, the Master
whispers "and the greatest of these is Love."

V, I have been entrusted to LOVE you, COVER you, RESTORE you and provide you a SAFE space. I'm here for it! I am here for it all. God gave us a covenant connection that transcends beyond failures or disappointments. For the only true failure is in not getting back up and fighting to be who God has called you to be. You don't owe me an apology. Truthfully, I cannot be more proud of you than I am in your ability to be transparent for the glory of God with this book.

I LOVE YOU!

Thank you for trusting me with your heart. I don't take that lightly, but at the same time, I always pray that God shows me how to respond when you open your heart and share. I value our open and honest relationship as all relationships need those two tenants for a solid foundation. Our conversations are not always easy but they are necessary for growth. They grow us both and I thank God for that. Though there are many days I am stretched beyond capacity, I realize that God uses our conversations to increase my faith and dependency on Him. I LOVE YOU!

It ain't no playbook written for the mother/daughter bond that we share. That was evident when you described the way love tastes and your lusts for a woman. Child, I just knew I had died and was in a holding place before entering heaven. I was shook! Do you hear me? I began to sweat because, for the first time probably ever, I was speechless. In that moment, you were too much and I needed to pray. Not just pray...lay before the Lord. Here's my transparency: "My daughter slept with a woman and uuuughhh yeah...I was a little rattled." I know that same sex relationships are out there but I didn't expect to have it show up at my door and in my face saying "hi".

WHAT?

Lord Jesus...Is this a real mother daughter issue or am I being punked? I ain't equipped for this! And I was tempted to address the details of the confessional especially the underwater oral. BUT the details don't matter in what I need to say. The details are your truth and I respect your truth! I LOVE YOU!

Baby, in no way do I condone what was done but it was done and I am past it. I just want to hug you, hug the little girl in you that has been tormented by her past for years. I am here with opened arms to welcome you home. There's nothing you have done that can separate you from the love of Christ and that's good enough for me. My arms are opened for you and I hold you in my heart. I pray for you when you're up and when you're down. I am your biggest cheerleader! You have etched a place in this world that's all yours and you own it. I'm here to love you always, to provide safety and reassurance when you need it, to cheer for you in every race and battle that you take on.

I am here to cover you and restore you. So, no matter how many times you fall in the dirt, I will be here to dust you off and tell you how brave and courageous you are, how beautiful you are, and how much I believe in you because I do. I believe in you! I am present and I am praying. I LOVE YOU!

My truth is I contemplated how to tackle this because the last thing I want to do is to be so heavenly minded that I am no earthly good. I have written and rewritten my response in my mind at least a hundred times. I am very concerned about my wording because it's not just a conversation between us but one for the world to listen to or read.

Nevertheless, God has commissioned me to be me. And in doing so, I give no power to where you've been or what you've done. I LOVE YOU! I love you unconditionally and you are mine. You will always be mine until God calls one of us home. I LOVE YOU!

It brings tears to my eyes to think of how deeply this ordeal has affected you...hurt you. I am hurt to know the pain this situation has caused you. Your willful participation in the relationship takes a backseat to the fact that you are my child and you experienced pain. And, with every fiber of my being I have compassion for that.

As I read and have heard your very raw emotions, I want to hug you, to comfort you and tell you that I love you unconditionally. I knew you were struggling as you still had unresolved issues within yourself that stemmed from childhood trauma. It was never about the details for me! And, despite all that has transpired, I love you! God graced me with you because He knew that He had equipped me with an unconditional love just for you. He knew that we'd make a great team. I'd love you unconditionally as if I'd birthed you myself. I'd cover you in prayer when you couldn't cover yourself. And I'd stick around when you tried to push me away. I am committed to showing up every day to be the consistent representative of God in your life. I LOVE YOU!

You remember the story of the prodigal son? When the son returned from squandering his inheritance, the father did not scorn him. Instead, the father embraced him, threw a party for him and outfitted him in the finest threads. He restored him and reminded him of his rightful place. I am here to remind you that you are fearfully and wonderfully made; that you're royalty, God's prized possession created in His likeness and image to bring Him glory. He loves you right where you are just the way you are.

I'm here to remind you of who you are in Him unapologetically and that all things work together for the good of those who love Him and are called according to His purpose. And you definitely are called to be a voice for such a time as this. Child, I love you so much! I know you have been stretched by sharing your truth. I, too, have been stretched in having to face the fact that my child hit the bottom and contemplated ending her life. Nobody wants to watch their child heartbroken. Yet, at the same time, I was praying .

"Lord, break her to make her!" And being at a distance not being able to wrap my arms around you immediately and tell you how much I love you was the worst. Therefore, I had to trust God to keep you. I couldn't physically touch you, I wasn't present and I was helpless. You, being at your lowest and me being helpless, I learned that my prayer life is stronger than your hopelessness and my helplessness combined. I had to surrender and call upon a Holy God who could penetrate your heart and mind. I prayed for the little girl in you searching to soothe her soul's trauma. Slowly, day by day, I watched God resuscitate you. He and He alone is who I praise for your life. I have experienced the scripture of God being my strength in weakness. He has given us LIFE! Shout about it!

In this very moment, I feel a shift, so allow me to shift into the presence of God. Child, you talked about soul ties and being tormented by them, feeling like your anointing is lost, restoration is out of reach and that you've failed your gifts by choosing sin.

STOP RIGHT THERE AND LET ME LOVE YOU!

For I started with God gave me love for you in the form of providing love, cover, restoration and safety. I must say this: REPENT!!! Have you repented? Have you laid it all before God and exposed every broken piece? I know that you have. Therefore, let me remind you of a few things. You are saved by your admitting you've sinned, believing that Jesus Christ is God's son and confessing your faith in Jesus Christ as your savior. Have I lost you yet? In other words, V, your salvation is enough to break the soul tie. Yep, I said it! Think about it! When we are consumed with the Savior who is our problem solver, we don't have time to dwell on the problem. It's not a problem when every time we think of the issue we seek God. Reference Matthew 6:33; But seek ye first the kingdom of God and His righteousness and all these things will be added unto you. Yes, a healed soul is included in there! You are reminded in Romans 11:29 that the gifts and calling are without repentance.

Repentance, in this context, means that God isn't going to recall the gift or change His mind concerning what He has called you to do. You have the choice to obey or not but the gift is still there. Pick it up and move forward! Pick it up and move forward!

Over in 2 Timothy, Paul told a young Timothy to "stir up the gift" of God. You have the fear and admonition of the Lord in your heart.

God has not taken His hands off of you,

nor turned a deaf ear to your earnest plea. Therefore, stir it up! Stir it up! Stir up the gift! Job 22:28 states; "Thou shalt also decree a thing and it will be established unto thee: and the light shall shine upon thy ways."

I make this declaration with the power given unto me by God through His word in the matchless name of Jesus.

I decree that you believe what the word of God says about you! V, you shall no longer carry word curses, negativity or any unlawful soul tie that the enemy has attached to you.

I decree that you will marry a God-fearing man who will love you as Christ loved the church and the two of you will be fruitful in everything you place your hands to do.

I decree that your family's ministry will be a life-changing, yoke destroying and soul prospering vehicle that will draw souls to Christ and His unconditional love.

I decree that you take your rightful place as heir and help me. You shall enjoy that which God does for you and through you.

I decree that you believe Jeremiah 1:5 that God knew you before He formed you. I decree you are sanctified and ordained a prophet.

I decree that you will meditate on that word daily. Because you were chosen before the foundation of the world, you will do as Habakkuk 2:2 states and write the vision and make it plain, through books, movies, songs and businesses.

I decree that you are a CEO that rules in righteousness providing excellent services and employing thousands of people. I decree that you will preach, teach, educate, motivate, stimulate, inspire, uplift and encourage the masses in the mighty name of Jesus. I decree that you maintain a strong faith and that suicide is not your portion. You shall live and not die and shall declare the works of the Lord always.

I decree in the majestic name of Jesus that you die to self, daily, and teach others that principle as you help them heal as YOU

ARE HEALED!

I decree that you will use the authority given to you to trample on snakes and scorpions and to overcome all the power of the enemy; nothing will harm you in Jesus' name. For you dwell in the shelter of the Most High and you rest in the shadow of the Almighty as stated in Psalm 91.

Glory to God in the highest!

Lastly, I decree 1 Peter 2:9 over you and ask that you declare it for yourself each day. I decree that

YOU ARE A CHOSEN VESSEL

YOU ARE ROYALTY

YOU ARE HOLY

YOU ARE GOD'S SPECIAL POSSESSION.

I decree that you may declare boldly the praises of him who called you out of darkness into His wonderful light.

VACHELLE S. JEMISON

YOU ARE RESTORED IN THE NAME OF JESUS!

My Suicide

I wanted my life to be a movie

It is compiled of all bad scenes

I wanted to wake up from this nightmare
Hoping this is only a bad dream

A little girl yearns for a father

Finding entrapment in penetrating lust

I wanted the ideal mother/daughter
relationship But ministry replaced the
mother's touch

I wanted to die loving one husband

But he, too, wanted a man

I just want to stand on the promise of God
Even when I can't see his plan

I'm not limited to my brokenness

But I want a mended broken heart

I want to trust loving again

Just don't know where I should start

I can't blame anyone for the things that I have experienced. I am definitely accepting responsibility. I recall a time when I thought I would get over being molested by my father. I was afraid of him, yet I loved him dearly. I knew it was toxic but I hoped and prayed that things would get better. After all this was my dad. What I never considered are the psychological affects that it would have on my adult life and how it would be a major influence in my ability to make decisions. I've made bad decisions trying to out run, out live, and even prove this had no power over me. Truth is I was hurting.

"The attacks of which I have been the object have broken the spring of life in me… People don't realize what it feels like to be constantly insulted".

Edward Manet

There is a broken girl inside
Wanting to love and love tends to hide
Gave my heart away so wrong
To hear about love through the phone
Long for the secret what may not be fate

I've given up on love and accepted broken
Re-breaking a broken heart has no hope

What was a secret trapped in the corner
dark space of my closet has now had some
breathe of life in it. When I was a little girl
everyone knew what life would hold in the
cards for me. Whether good or bad, they had
a vision concerning who I was, where I was
going, how I would be nothing, some called
me dumb while others called me smart. Some
called me beautiful while others were certain
I would never be loved with my ugly self. I
used to wonder how they knew. I used to
wonder if I was finally ready to accept their
versions of who I am. I learned I was making
a promise to myself to receive the brokenness
spoken over me and make it my own. If I
wasn't broken, I became broken by trying to
prove to everyone that they were wrong
about me.

I had fake smiles to go with my fake friends
and my real family with fake love. I took the
negativity they spoke over me as my own. I
took ownership of what was never mine to
have and allowed it to fester over the tears.
Now, this negativity that I took as my own
was growing, but I was failing to feed my

spirit man. What happens when you become malnourished but there is great growth from the troubles that are surrounding you? When there is no one there to help you from your fallen place? Two are better than one, because they have a good return for their labor: If either of them falls down, one can help the other up. But pity anyone who falls and has no one to help them up. Also, if two lie down together, they will keep warm.

But how can one keep warm alone? Though one may be overpowered, two can defend themselves. A cord of three strands is not quickly broken.

An even bigger question is what happens when there are two walking in agreement and fall together? Is it possible to fall with the person whom you feel was GOD sent to walk in purpose with you?

Can you overcome?

Sitting in the car in that parking lot was definitely not the beginning of trouble and not the beginning of suicidal thoughts. It was the pressure build-up that was finally too much. There had been no release of pressure in some time. I have been carrying trouble since I was 12 years old, and only letting just enough to go that it didn't take my life.

Have we not all at some point had a David experience in the thirty-eighth Psalms? My guilt has overwhelmed me like a burden too heavy to bear. I have had one too many of these over the last ten years, but if I were honest with myself, the moments are not multiple moments. What appears to be multiple moment are the after effects of unhealed past pain. What happens when you take problems and pack them into a box to deal with them later and because other things are more pressing later never comes? Now, you're faced with ten years' worth of later to deal with/ I'll deal with that tomorrow.

Tomorrow has not arrived. Not by choice, but the list of things to do tomorrow has become too much to have packed in such a small space. Things that are spilling and these compartmentalized issues are becoming cross contaminated. There is a huge mess. Ah - but this is not a typical mess - this is my life. The adversity is different.

It could clean and make whole.

Healing Not Easy!

Mother, this for us has been a ride. Look at this therapeutic session that we have just had. I appreciate having a safe space where I can reveal who Vachelle is. Far too long, I've been in a box or on a pedestal and I'm over it. I'm tired of living in the shadows of what someone's ideals of whom I should be. I'm over it. By the age of thirty-two, I found that I was just inexperienced as I've been living voraciously through everyone's definition of me. I've spent nearly my entire adulthood people-pleasing. My walk in Christianity has been with a good heart but some of it has just been to prove others wrong. Though I pushed you away a thousand times, two thousand times, you came back and loved me anyway.

You allowed me to pull off the mask, and for that, I am forever grateful.

It's so funny looking at your transparent moment because I was asking myself the same things in the moment. Jesus, am I being punked? Am I equipped for this? I don't want to be here. I really don't want to be here but the head this woman gives has me rethinking my entire life right now. I mean, with a mouth like hers, how can this be a blessing unto me and a so much sin at the same time? GOD, take me from this. I really don't want it and I don't want to be distracted by how this makes me feel. Everything good to you is not good for you. It's in the perfect moment of being welcomed home that I find my suicide. I find my earnest yes to the death of everything outside of the will of GOD concerning me. I say yes to death. Yes to the crucifixion of what was.

My heart leaps at the thought of knowing the cheering in this instance is not for cheering for me to fail. Your voice is not etched into my mental with the words of disappointment and feeling not good enough for you. You chose to mother me and replace the years of feeling as if I should have been aborted. One cannot fathom how difficult is it wanting to die because people treat you as if you are dead already. All these church folks got me feeling like the woman awaiting to be stoned because those around her had forgotten they were not perfect. Church is for sinners like them but not sinners like me.

I'm grateful for your compassion. I don't know what was worse, the guilt I felt because I fell or telling my "leader" I messed up and the moments of rejection and lack of empathy in my moment of weakness and honesty. I almost took a back seat to being a Christian because I didn't want to serve people with the mindset of the Sadducees. Condemnation doesn't lead people to Christ nor does it help the fallen to stand again. Maybe it was tough love. Whatever it was, I'm glad that it's not what you gave to me. You didn't overwhelm me with it.

Bless the Lord that I'm not constantly reliving my past mistakes and you opened a door for healing - it is because the details never mattered that I was transparent. I was beating myself up enough and didn't need the "that was your faults" and the "you knew betters". If I am "confessing" I was wrong, then I am acknowledging that I knew better.

I definitely remember the parable of the prodigal son. After time in therapy and taking things one day at a time, I threw a party to celebrate. No, the pain had not gone away and at this point, I had charged this pain to being a thorn in my flesh. Truth is she chose me and I was a consenting participant to be outside of the will of GOD. It feels good to have DIED to self. This process was hard. This lesson was hard. The greatest gift of them all was understanding love in its fullness - the patience, kindness, long suffering, not easily angered. The hard one though was keeps no record of wrong. How do I not keep records of being told you were paid to tell the job I wanted to kill you? Your complaints of harassment and you were living in my house? Keep no record of being forced to be strong because you are not the favorite child? Keep no record. How GOD?

DEATH

It is well with my soul.

!!!SURRENDER!!!

Who can cry for the little girl once lost and all alone; abandoned without her own. The little girl from this broken place has many nights cried herself to sleep. But bless the Lord for a Holy Ghost that lives inside of me. Wanting to end it all from years of being overwhelmed and never speaking a mumbling word. This is the potter's wheel and it's not for the weak. To think that the enemy conspired with loved ones and it caused me to bend but not break. I was traumatized. But like David, I had to encourage myself.

Praise HIM! Worthy is the Lamb that was slain. It was the declaration of the Lord that I would live and not die declaring HIS works. I had to die that I might live. Hear me when I say suicide is not the answer. There is another way - GOD's way.

Mother,
I love you to the moon. You are a God's best for me. The tormenting was over the top. Knowing that I failed myself and I could hear this woman's voice in my sleep telling me to kill myself. This Jezebel has me no more. No longer can she distract me from the move that she was calling

me to. This has nothing to do with the faces that have hurt me to this point, but the "spirit" that has used them all. I shout loudly from the mountain top to those struggling BREATHE!!!

GOD's GOT THIS.

This experience has taught me the power of soul ties. The power of giving yourself to someone not just your body, but emotional and spiritual. Spiritually, sin consumes in ways that I cannot find adjectives to describe. BUT GOD, having to lie before God naked with my HERE I AM flaws and all; my mistakes; and honestly presenting him with it- healing comes. Not the kind of healing where you have to avoid the people that betrayed you, but the kind that allows you to stare them right in the face and say thank you, I love you, I forgive you. I give charge to those holding pain- forgive. Not for them but all those that are waiting for you to help them.

I am grateful that you are always praying for me when I am doing right or when I have been distracted from doing right. The power of the spoken word. As you have decreed, I sat my heart in expectation and agreement beyond me, but for all those who are reading that has had life trauma push them into suicidal thoughts.

Curse breaking	Amen
Renouncing soul ties	Amen

Wait, you kind of lost me with this one right here concerning me, but I believe it for all that reads who desire (Lord whatever your will be my soul says yes)

God fearing [wo]man	Amen
Fruitful in all I touch	Amen
Teach me to lift my children before you that they walk according to you will	
	Amen
Adjusting my crown	Amen
Jeremiah 1:5 confirmed	Amen

Discipline for daily meditation	Amen
Flowing through the pen	Amen
CEO	Amen
Flowing in my gifts	Amen
Psalms 91	Amen
1 Peter 2:9	Amen

My heart is set in expectation to receive all that God has in store, even the things that I don't know I can accomplish.

I am binding the spirit of suicide in Jesus name. I am believing God for the miracles of those who read. I believe that your pain will push you into purpose like never before. I believe that you will birth what you were born to do because of this hurt. I am believing God that you will forgive the apology that may never come. I had to do this myself. You are stronger than you think, and I completely understand that pain doesn't go away overnight, but when properly redirected you become some kind of superhero.

VACHELLE S. JEMISON

I will not die, but live,

And tell of the works of the LORD!!!

This is My Suicide that I die daily that I might live in Christ.

Grace~ Peace~ and Blessings!

VACHELLE S. JEMISON

Other Books

By

Vachelle S. Jemison

His Woman, His Wife; Her Lover, Her Lord:
The Art of Marriage

A Victim's Victory

Made in the USA
Columbia, SC
07 March 2024